CW00403643

# A plan for reducing the poor's-rate, by giving permanent employment to the labouring classes: with some observations on the cultivation of flax and hemp; and an account of a new process for dressing and preparing flax and hemp, without water-steeping or d

Hill, Samuel, Esq

BIBLIOLIFE

**Copyright © BiblioLife, LLC**

This historical reproduction is part of a unique project that provides opportunities for readers, educators and researchers by bringing hard-to-find original publications back into print at reasonable prices. Because this and other works are culturally important, we have made them available as part of our commitment to protecting, preserving and promoting the world's literature. These books are in the "public domain" and were digitized and made available in cooperation with libraries, archives, and open source initiatives around the world dedicated to this important mission.

We believe that when we undertake the difficult task of re-creating these works as attractive, readable and affordable books, we further the goal of sharing these works with a global audience, and preserving a vanishing wealth of human knowledge.

Many historical books were originally published in small fonts, which can make them very difficult to read. Accordingly, in order to improve the reading experience of these books, we have created "enlarged print" versions of our books. Because of font size variation in the original books, some of these may not technically qualify as "large print" books, as that term is generally defined; however, we believe these versions provide an overall improved reading experience for many.

A

# PLAN

FOR

## REDUCING THE POOR'S-RATE,

BY GIVING

### PERMANENT EMPLOYMENT

TO THE

## Labouring Classes:

WITH

SOME OBSERVATIONS ON THE CULTIVATION OF
FLAX AND HEMP;

AND

AN ACCOUNT OF A NEW PROCESS FOR DRESSING AND
PREPARING FLAX AND HEMP, WITHOUT WATER-
STEEPING OR DEW-ROTTING.

### BY SAMUEL HILL, ESQ.

WITH

THE REPORT OF A COMMITTEE OF THE HOUSE OF
COMMONS

ON THE MERITS OF THE INVENTION.

SECOND EDITION.

LONDON:

PRINTED FOR J. HARDING, 36, ST. JAMES'S-STREET;
By B. M'Millan, Bow-Street, Covent-Garden.

1817.

[*Price One Shilling.*]

# PREFACE.

When an individual recommends the Public to adopt a measure which would be serviceable to himself, he has no right to complain, should his sincerity be suspected; but I must beg it may be recollected, that I might easily have sheltered myself from this suspicion under an assumed name. Yet, as I can only expect success from the eligibility of the measure which I have to propose, I prefer openly avowing myself to be a Proprietor of the Machines, as well as the proposer of the Plan in which they are recommended; and I am also induced to make this avowal, with a view to facilitate enquiries into a project, from the adoption of which I sincerely believe the most permanent advantages would result to the country. I am therefore anxious to court investigation, and shall be glad to give any further explanation of my

Plan, and of the Machines, on which its pro-
fitableness and fitness must depend.

I have visited the numerous Poor-houses
in London and its vicinity, and it was from
personal observation of the situation of the
Poor, both within and without those walls,
that I became convinced of the expediency,
and I may add, charity, of supplying them
with easy and profitable employment. This
opinion has since been confirmed, by the
perusal of Baron Von Voght's excellent account of the management of the Poor of
Hamburgh, where, by means nearly similar
to those I intend to propose, the state of the
Poor, from being the worst, became the best
regulated of any city in Europe.

I have inserted a particular description of
the Machines, and an estimate of the value
and quantity of material which can be produced by using them. They are now worked
at a manufactory within the distance of a
mile from London, where any one inclined
to inspect them, may have an opportunity.

Several gentlemen of the highest respectability have already taken that trouble; they were twice shewn at the Royal Institution, and were again sent for, to be examined before Lord Spencer, and a Select Committee assembled for the purpose. In every instance, I have been gratified by receiving the unqualified approbation of the inspectors.

The Governors of the New Penitentiary have directed them to be used in that prison; and they have been already ordered for the Poor-houses in several parishes.

The Right Honourable President of the Royal Society, Sir Joseph Banks, whose experience and superior judgment in every branch of science and the useful arts, are so universally acknowledged, inspected the first Machines that were made, and I am authorized by his kind favor, to express his full and entire approbation of them.

SAMUEL HILL.

*No. 13, Montague Street,*
  *Portman Square,*
   *28th April,* 1817.

A

# PLAN,

*&c.* *&c.*

---

THAT the present distress of the Poor of these kingdoms arises from want of employment, though a deplorable fact, is now universally admitted. To dwell upon the numerous causes which have concurred to produce this evil, would be unnecessary; but a plan to remedy or alleviate suffering, is deserving the consideration of every humane and reflecting mind; and, as an individual who feels, in common with every Englishman, for the distresses of his countrymen, I address myself without apology to His Majesty's Ministers, and the Members of the Legislature; feeling confident they will cheerfully give their attention to any plan which may appear likely to restore internal comfort to the country: and trusting that their sanction will not be refused to the measures I may have to propose, if found worthy of their support.

I should indeed feel diffident in recommending an *untried* plan, but as a similar one has been practised at Hamburgh for years, with the completest success, and under circumstances of much greater difficulty, little apprehension of disappointment need be entertained.

In England, much is already done; age, sickness, infancy, all are provided for in the numerous and excellent Asylums, Hospitals, and Schools. Funds, much greater than what ought to be sufficient, are raised by the Poor's-rate, but a better distribution of them is required. I beg leave to be permitted to point out some of the most obvious defects of the present system of Poor-houses, which render them, in many instances, an unmerited recompense, and an undeserved punishment.

By the present Laws, the idle and profligate are as much entitled to relief, as the honest and industrious; and the salutary dread of starving, the only motive powerful enough to force such wretches to labour, is removed.

On the other hand, how hard is the lot of those who ask only employment, and cannot obtain it! Guilty of no crime, but poverty, they are driven from their humble cottages into the Parish Poor-house, to herd with the lowest and most disgraced of the human species; and their children to contamination, by associating with vice! What must be the sufferings of a spirit once independent? It must soon break, or become callous to every virtuous and respectable feeling. If a plan can be devised to avert such misery, will not humanity rejoice, and promote it with ardour? Such a plan is not only practicable, but easy, on that excellent principle of sound policy and true charity—that employment, and not alms, should be given to all who have any ability to work, however small their capability may be.

On this admirable principle, I hope to be able to show, how the Poor may live at all times upon the earnings of their own industry; the worthless be prevented from preying in idleness upon a benevolent public; and the country be relieved from the heavy and almost insupportable weight of Poor's-rates.

To effect these happy purposes, Parish Manufactories should be established, where all who ask employment, or relief, may be set to work. They should be in *totally distinct Buildings* from the Parish Poor-houses, which ought to be appropriated solely to those who are incapable of doing any thing towards their maintenance. These Manufactories would be a certain resource to the labourer, at those seasons when other employment could not be had ; and after the labours of the day, he might then return to his fire-side, and to peaceful rest with his family. Those whose distresses arise only from a temporary want of employment, would be rescued from that degrading sense of dependence, which has frequently so injurious an effect upon the character, as to discourage any future attempt to become industrious and respectable. Thus is an useful member of society worse than lost ; he becomes a burthen, if not a scourge.

The establishment I should think the best calculated, is a Manufactory for the purpose of dressing and preparing Flax and Hemp, and spinning and weaving the thread and yarn. My reasons for recommending it are, as follow :

1st, The growth of the materials, and the

manufacturing and consumption of them, are within our own country; consequently they may always be procured, and are always saleable.

2nd, All the processes previous to spinning, viz. breaking, rubbing, and hackling, are now rendered so simple, by the use of the patent machinery, as to require no instruction, and very little strength; therefore women, children, aged and infirm persons, incapable and unaccustomed to any other kind of labour, may thus be employed.

3rd, The remaining processes of spinning and weaving, are exactly adapted to that class of persons now most destitute; the silk-weavers of Spitalfields, and the cotton-weavers in general.

4th, This sort of manufactory would require little trouble in overlooking and managing; as the material may be weighed or measured to and from the labourer, and consequently there could be no fraud.

5th, Very little capital would be required, the raw material being cheap—any vacant building might be rented for the purpose— the hire of the Patent Machines is moderate, and looms and spinning-wheels may be had upon very reasonable terms.

6th, The profits are so considerable, that not only all those able to work, might be advantageously employed, but there would remain a considerable surplus in aid of the support of those who are incapable of labour.

It is here necessary to give some account of the Patent Machines, which, by their introducing a new mode of preparing Flax and Hemp, will not only render it a profitable and rapid trade to the manufacturer, and consequently reduce the price of those articles to the consumer, but the cultivation of these crops will become very beneficial to the Proprietor, as well as to the Occupier of the Soil.

The machines are constructed to perform three progressive processes, so as to complete the material for the spinner, which may be worked by them into the finest state possible, equal to that used in France and the Netherlands for the finest lace and cambrick. The machines do not require fixing, and are light enough to be easily removed*.

Six of these machines, viz. two breakers, two rubbers, and two for the purpose of hackling, may be so attached, that two men may turn them with great ease.

* The dimensions of the largest machine, are only three feet long by two feet wide, and four feet in height.

The two breakers require the attention of two boys or women to each machine. One boy or woman can supply two rubbing machines, and one boy or woman can attend two hackling machines ; in all, eight persons, who with these six machines, which are adapted to take the work from each other in succession, would be able to complete one ton of the stem of Flax from the field, fit for the use of the spinner, in five days.

*First Cost of a Ton of Stem of Flax, and Expenses in Working, by the New Process.*

| | £ | s | d |
|---|---|---|---|
| One ton purchased at 5l. 5s. which price will allow an ample profit to the grower, | £5 | 5 | 0 |
| Hire of two pair of machines, at 10s. per day, | 2 | 10 | 0 |
| Hire of two hackling-machines, .................... | 0 | 15 | 0 |
| Wages of two men, at 1s. 6d. each per day, | 0 | 15 | 0 |
| Wages of six boys, at 10d. each per day, | 1 | 5 | 0 |
| | £10 | 10 | 0 |

That workmen may not be encouraged to quit their masters, nor the parish manufactory be overstocked with hands, it would be advisable that the wages should be something below the general rate of the country. They are accordingly calculated very moderately in this estimate.

A ton of the stem of Flax is reduced by the

processes of the breaking and rubbing machines, to 5 cwt. at 112 lb. per cwt. of the fibre, which the new process of hackling separates into flax and tow, in the proportion of two-thirds flax and one-third tow.

*Value of Produce completed for the Spinner.*

| | | | |
|---|---|---|---|
| 373 lbs. of flax, at 1s. per pound, ............ | £18 | 13 | 0 |
| 187 lbs. of tow, at 6d. per pound, ................ | 4 | 13 | 6 |
| | £23 | 6 | 6 |
| Deduct expenses, and first cost of a ton of material in the stem, ........................ | 10 | 10 | 0 |
| Profit, ...................................... | £12 | 16 | 6 |

As the processes of spinning and weaving linen cloth are generally known, it is only necessary for me to state, that 5 cwt. of the fibre of flax, prepared according to the estimate, into flax and tow, will spin into 560 lbs. of yarn, which, when woven (the average calculation being half a pound of yarn to one yard of linen), will make 1120 yards of yard-wide linen of good strong quality, worth 2s. per yard in the shops. The value of a pound of the flax is generally allowed for spinning a pound of yarn, and 6d. per yard is the average price of weaving. The account of the expenses and profit, when spun and woven, will therefore be as follows:

### Expenses.

| | | | |
|---|---|---|---|
| Spinning 373lbs. of flax, at 1s. per pound*, | £18 | 13 | 0 |
| Spinning 187 lbs. of tow, at 8d. .................. | 6 | 4 | 8 |
| Weaving 1120 yards of linen, at 6d. per } yard, ........................................} | 28 | 0 | 0 |
| | £52 | 17 | 8 |
| Add the first cost of one ton of stem, and } the expenses in working, as per former } statement, ......................................} | 10 | 10 | 0 |
| | £63 | 7 | 8 |

### Value of Produce when Spun and Woven.

| | | | |
|---|---|---|---|
| 1120 yards of linen cloth, at 2s. per yard, | £112 | 0 | 0 |
| Deduct the cost of material and labour, } as above, .........................................} | 63 | 7 | 8 |
| Clear profit, ...................... | £48 | 12 | 4 |

It appears then, that the manufacturing of a single ton of flax from the stem, will produce a clear profit of 48l. 12s. 4d. besides expending 54l. 17s. 8d. in labour.

* The price allowed for spinning and weaving are sufficiently ample to include the expense of washing with soap and water, which will render the yarn and linen perfectly white, without bleaching.

The advantages of such employment will be still more evident, and the enormous amount of Poor's-rates seem less extraordinary, when it is understood that the general rate of earnings in Poor-houses, do not exceed one halfpenny per day. One hundred and fifty persons capable of labour, in St. Giles's Poor-house (as appears from the books), earned by picking oakum, in the year ending at Lady-day 1817, 72*l*. 4*s*. 6*d*. which, after deducting the per centage of the Master of the Poor-house, and the wages of the Overlooker, would not amount to one halfpenny per day for each person.

The majority of the inhabitants of Poor-houses are capable of supporting themselves, and could the system I have been endeavouring to recommend, be acted upon, the Poor's-rates in all probability would soon be unnecessary. The calculation of the profits which would arise, appears to be incredible, until the difference of the *produce,* and other advantages of the new process, are compared with the old methods of dressing and preparing flax and hemp.

## The Old Process.

The old methods of dew-rotting and water-steeping, which prepare the fibre for separation by fermentation and decay, destroy the useful qualities of every other particle of the plant. Neither sustenance for animals is afforded, nor return of manure made to the soil. On this account, crops of flax or hemp are frequently prohibited by Landed Proprietors. The effects of these processes are also so injurious to the fibre, that only one-tenth or eleventh part of serviceable flax can be obtained from a ton of the stem, *half of which* becomes tow when hackled, and the expense of preparing it for the spinner, including hackling, is 1*l.* 17*s.* 4*d.* per cwt. The loss of time is another objection: these processes cannot be completed under two or three months. Five or six weeks more are wasted in the operation of bleaching, a process very detrimental to the strength of the linen, (from the chemical acids generally used), but which is necessary to remove the dark gray stain which the flax acquires from the moisture and decay to which the plant is exposed. The expense of bleaching is also very heavy.

### The New Process.

The new Patent Machines separate the fibre without wasting any part of the plant, which may be ascertained by weighing; the land will therefore be as much benefited by this crop as any other, the chaff (gluten and woody parts of the plant) is an excellent food for cattle, and from its oily nature, is even in itself a good manure.

All the fibre which the plant contains, about one-fourth of the whole substance, is preserved with its natural strength unimpaired; one-fourth, or 5 cwt. of fibre being obtained from a ton of the stem, which can be prepared and hackled for the spinner at 21s. per cwt. including the hire of the Patent Machines. The process of hackling separates the fibre into two-thirds of flax and only one-third of tow.

The several processes, from the time the plant is harvested to the delivery of the flax to the spinner, may be completed in a few hours. No bleaching is required, for the yellow appearance of the flax, which is merely gluten, is easily removed by soap and water.

This comparison shews, that nearly three times more fibre is gained by the new process than by the old method, and at less than *half the expense.*

From returns made, it appears that 93,000 acres of flax and hemp were last year grown in Ireland, and 16,500 acres in Scotland. The number of acres cultivated for these purposes in England, cannot be exactly ascertained; but it may not be unreasonable to estimate them at 10,500 statute acres, making in the whole 120,000 acres. As the Irish and Scotch acre is considerably larger than the English, the average produce of an acre may be calculated at three tons of stem per acre; the total quantity of flax produced will be 360,000 tons. From this quantity of stem there would only be obtained, by the *old method* of preparation, one-eleventh part of the fibre, or 32,727 tons; while, by the *new process*, one-fourth part is obtained, amounting to 90,000 tons. The difference of 57,273 tons of fibre, saved by the new process, would produce an increase of 256,583,040 yards of linen, which, valued at an average of

2s. per yard, would be a clear profit to the country of 25,658,304*l. from the same number of acres employed;* and the manufacturing of the additional quantity of material, would give employment to 781,622 persons, averaging their wages at 1s. per day, as two-thirds of them would be women and boys. This increase of wealth to the country, and employment to the people, would result from the land at present under the cultivation of flax and hemp; and when it is considered that our population are asking employment, while large tracts of our lands are lying barren, and Foreigners are enriching themselves in our markets, by cultivating and manufacturing a plant so well calculated to be grown on our own soil, is it unreasonable to suppose that our Government will gladly encourage and protect such a plan?

The necessary encouragement I conceive would be given, on the exclusion of foreign flax, hemp, and linen from our ports; by imposing additional duties, (the present duty on flax is very small), and by inducing individuals to take into cultivation those parts of our extensive wastes which are well adapted to the growth of flax and hemp. Great profit might also be derived to Government from cultivating these crops upon the Crown Lands, for the service of the Navy.

The discovery of a simple method of preparing our raw materials, so as to enable us to rival the finest and most durable fabricks of the Continent, again offers us that extensive trade and commerce which a change from War to Peace has diminished. We have an immense consumption within our own country, and in our Colonies: we may now provide our ships with the best canvas and cordage, and be no longer dependent on a foreign nation for our maritime supplies.

So many able pens have been engaged in recommending employment, as the only judicious mode of relieving the difficulties which every class of the community suffer, that I should not have obtruded my opinions, did I not believe that the Plan which I have suggested, would afford permanent relief. And when I reflect upon the exertions which have been made by the higher ranks of society, to alleviate the wants of the people, and the anxiety with which the Representatives of the Country are now endeavouring to establish a mode of permanent relief, I am encouraged to think that a Plan, formed upon much observation and reflection, and the estimates, which have been made with great care and every possible exactness, may not be unacceptable.

## On the Cultivation of Flax and Hemp.

To a few observations on these crops, I beg to call the attention of the Landed Proprietor, whose interest will be more benefited by promoting the cultivation of them, than any other member of the community, both as the possessor of the soil, and as a contributor to the Poor's-rates, which I have endeavoured to shew, may be much reduced by the employment which these crops would afford. And if the new process of preparing the fibre, renders them more productive in value, and more beneficial in their effects to the soil, than crops generally cultivated, they consequently must increase the value of the land, and the Farmer will be able to afford a better rent.

Flax and hemp remain so short a time in the ground, that they cannot be very exhausting; and from their rapid growth, they quickly cover the surface and keep down the weeds.

All overshadowing vegetables, by preventing the moisture of the earth from being evaporated by the heat of the sun, are known from experience to render it more fertile ; and that flax and hemp are really not impoverishing crops, is still better proved by the practice in every country where they are grown, of sowing wheat after them. It is the common husbandry on the banks of the Garonne, and in the Bolognese, as well as in our own counties of Suffolk, Lincolnshire, and Yorkshire. Yet as the old methods of separating the fibre, by dew-rotting and water-steeping, destroy the nutritive qualities of the plant, as food for cattle, the consequent loss of manure to the soil, justified the Landlord in discouraging the cultivation.

The new process has, however, completely removed these objections, for as the fibre is separated from the plant by the Machines in the same state of freshness as it comes from the field, the nutritious qualities of the chaff cannot be impaired ; and with the seed, as much and as valuable food for cattle is obtained, as from a crop of oats ; therefore the quantity of nutriment will not be diminished, however extended the culture of flax and hemp may become; but, on the contrary, increased, as the cleanness of the cultivation enables the Farmer to follow it with wheat, the next most profitable crop, which cannot be sown with success after oats or barley.

Those lands which are calculated for oats or barley, are well suited to flax : the time of sowing is from the middle of March to the latter end of April. When the soil is well ploughed and made fine by harrowing and rolling, the seed should then be sown broad-cast; and as the finest stems produce the most valuable fibre, it is advisable to sow the seed thick ; the usual quantity is two and a half or three bushels per acre.

The crop should be kept perfectly clean by weeding, until the plants are five or six inches high, but should not afterwards be disturbed, nor will it be necessary, as the plants are then strong enough to prevent the growth of weeds.

About August, the stem generally turns yellow, the seed is formed in the pods, and it is then ready to be harvested.

The plants should be pulled up and laid upon the ground, in bundles as large as can be grasped in both hands, where they should re-main until the upper part of the stems are dry, which they will be in fine weather in a couple

of days. The bundles, with the root ends of
the plants laid even, should then be made up,
and set in shocks of ten bundles each (with
the dry ends of the plants turned to the in-
side) until the pods and every part of the
stem are perfectly dry. They will then be
ready to be worked, housed, or stacked; if
stacked, the root ends should be placed on the
outside, and the stack should be well thatched.

Hemp requires a stronger and richer soil;
but the management and profits of the crop
are nearly the same. Both these crops are
well suited to new soils, and the Farmer's
expense in cultivating them, upon such wastes
as are worth enclosing, will be well repaid.
An acre generally yields two tons and a half
of stem, which will contain about fourteen
bushels of seed ; the present value of a ton of
stem, is 5l. 5s. and the seed is worth 10s. 6d.
per bushel.

|  | £ | s. | d. |
|---|---|---|---|
| Two tons and a half of stem, at 5l. 5s. per ton, | 13 | 2 | 6 |
| Fourteen bushels of seed, at 10s. 6d. per bushel, | 7 | 7 | 0 |
|  | £20 | 9 | 6 |

The new mode of preparing flax, is as simple, and may be as easily understood, as the preparation of wheat for the mill. The Farmer would find it extremely advantageous to adopt this process, as it will leave the chaff and refuse to be consumed upon his farm, and give employment to his men, when the weather will not permit their labours in the field. The profits will amply repay his trouble and expense, as exhibited in the annexed Table.

## A Calculation of the Value of the Produce and the Expense, of Cultivating and Preparing an Acre of Flax fit for Market.

### EXPENSES, per Acre.

| | £ | s. | d. |
|---|---|---|---|
| Rent, taxes, and tythe, - - - | 2 | 10 | 0 |
| Ploughing, - - - - | 0 | 15 | 0 |
| Harrowing and rolling, - - - | 0 | 10 | 0 |
| Three bushels of seed for sowing, - - | 1 | 11 | 6 |
| Weeding, - - - - | 0 | 10 | 0 |
| Pulling, - - - - | 1 | 0 | 0 |
| Stacking, - - - - | 0 | 10 | 0 |
| Threshing 1¾ bushels of seed, at 1s. per bushel, | 0 | 14 | 0 |
| The hire of a pair of patent machines, at 10s. per cwt. | 6 | 5 | 0 |
| Labour in working the two machines, at 5s. per cwt. | 3 | 2 | 6 |
| | £17 | 8 | 0 |

### PRODUCE, per Acre.

| | £ | s. | d. |
|---|---|---|---|
| Two tons and a half of stem, when prepared by the new improved machines, will produce 12¼ cwt. of flax, which is one fourth, valued at 63s. per cwt. - | £39 | 7 | 6 |
| Fourteen bushels of seed, at 10s. 6d. per bushel, | 7 | 7 | 0 |
| Ninety-eight bushels of chaff, from the seed for horses, at 6d. per bushel, - | 2 | 9 | 0 |
| 37½ cwt. of chaff from the stem of the flax, for cattle, at 1s. per cwt. - - | 1 | 17 | 6 |
| | £51 | 1 | 0 |
| Deduct expenses, - - - - | 17 | 8 | 0 |
| Net profit per acre, - - - - | £33 | 13 | 0 |

A Patent for breaking flax and hemp without dew-retting, was granted some years ago, but was not found to answer to the full extent expected. The same work is now performed by the new patent machines at 100 per cent. less expense, without injury to the fibre, and with a saving in the material.

# PETITION

TO THE

## HOUSE OF COMMONS,

AND

### REPORT OF COMMITTEE ON IT.

———————

*Lunæ, 12° die Maii, 1817.*

A Petition of Samuel Hill and William
Bundy, of Camden Town, in the County of
Middlesex, joint Proprietors of certain Machines for preparing Flax and Hemp in the dry
state from the stem, without undergoing the
usual long process of dew-rotting or water-
steeping, for which the said parties have obtained His Majesty's Letters Patent, was pre-
sented and read; setting forth, that the Petitioners, after great expense and much labour,
have discovered a process, by rendering certain
Machinery subservient to manual labour, of
breaking and preparing Flax and Hemp in a
dry state from the stems of the said plants, su-
perseding the necessity of dew-rotting or water-
steeping, and that by these means nearly three
times more of the fibrous parts, uninjured by
fermentation and decay, are obtained from the

same produce per acre, at half the expense,
and in a less number of hours, than has hither-
to required weeks by the old method ; that, to
effect this purpose, the stems of Flax and Hemp,
when dry from the field or stack, are passed
through two Machines, the first called a
Breaker, the second a Rubber, after which it
is completed for spinning by a third, which
performs the operation of heckling, all which
being of a portable construction, the largest
requiring the space of three feet by four only,
are well calculated for giving employment to
cottagers, and the lower orders of the people
at their own homes, as also to the labour of
paupers in workhouses, and convicts in prisons,
and penitentiaries, and houses of correction;
that by the Petitioners' improved process, much
time and expense are saved, while the deterio-
rating effects of bleaching are obviated, as
Flax, Hemp, and Tow, thus prepared, are rendered equally white and fit for use, by washing
in soap and water only; that, from the Petitioners' improved mode of preparation, the additional quantity of Flax, Hemp, and Tow,
which would be procured from the 120,000
acres supposed to be employed in the cultivation of these crops in Ireland, Scotland, and
England, would afford an increase of employment in the several operations of preparing,

spinning, weaving, and washing, to upwards
of 700,000 persons, and an additional annual
return of 25,000,000*l.* when manufactured into
Linen ; that besides these advantages derivable
by the Farmer and the Manufacturer, the general prejudice entertained by the landholders
against the growth of these crops would be
removed, as the chaff produced in the operations of breaking and rubbing, is found to be
excellent food for cattle, and would consequently, like that of other crops, make a due
return to the soil in the shape of manure ; that
the Petitioners humbly presume to be of opinion, that a general adoption of their process
would greatly increase the produce of the
crops of Flax and Hemp, and consequently the
value of the land in Great Britain, and particu-
larly in Ireland, and in the course of a few
years, render the country wholly independent
of Foreign States for these Naval Supplies ;
and the Petitioners humbly conceive that their
invention may be of great National importance,
in the cultivation of waste lands by the plough
or the spade, and of great domestic relief, in affording constant employment to many thousands
of the labouring classes, at that season of the
year when out-door work is difficult to be procured ; and they humbly request, that the
House will be pleased to afford them an oppor-

tunity of proving these their allegations, before a Select Committee of the House appointed for that purpose, in order that the attention of the Nation may be called to an object of such internal political consequence.

---

# REPORT

*From Committee on Petitions relating to Machinery for Manufacturing of Flax.*

The Committee to whom the Petition of Samuel Hill and William Bundy, and also the Petition of James Lee, were referred; to report the same, with their Observations thereupon, to the House;—have examined several Witnesses in support of the Allegations of the said Petitions; and agreed upon the following Report:

" Your Committee, in obedience to the directions of the House, proceeded to take into consideration the Petition of Messrs. Hill and Bundy, on their improved method of preparing Flax and Hemp, in a dry state, from the stem, without undergoing the former process of water-steeping or dew-rotting.

E

" Your Committee received satisfactory proof, that the preparing Flax and Hemp, in a dry state, for Spinning, answered most completely, and was likely to prove a great and valuable improvement, both to the grower and manufacturer; the cost of preparing being less; avoiding the risk of steeping, which is considerable; a great saving also in time and material.

" It was proved also to your Committee, that the strength and quality of Cloth manufactured from Flax thus prepared, are much superior to that produced from Flax which has been water-steeped or dew-rotted.

" Your Committee are fully impressed with the great national advantages likely to result from this discovery, by which it would appear, that a saving in the proportion of ninety to thirty-three would be obtained on the annual growth of Flax in the Empire, computed at 120,000 acres, affording an increase of employment to many thousands, and an augmentation of the national wealth to the amount of many millions, as will more fully appear by reference to the evidence in corroboration of the allegations set forth by the said Petitioners.

" It appeared also in evidence before your Committee, that the Flax prepared by Messrs.

Hill and Bundy's Machines, was superior to any dew-rotted Flax; and that large orders had already been given for Flax thus prepared, by the house of Messrs. Benyon and Co. at Leeds, one of the most considerable manufacturers of Flax in the kingdom.

" Your Committee proceeded also to the consideration of the Petition of James Lee, but did not feel themselves competent to go into any examination of the allegations, stating an infringement of Mr. Lee's Patent. As far as the evidence before the Committee was adduced, it did not seem to justify such an assumption. This, however, is a question for a Court of Law.

" Evidence on the part of Mr. Lee, was produced to your Committee, to shew Mr. Lee's Machines were in use, in various Workhouses, in different parts of the Kingdom : That Mr. Lee's manner of preparing Flax was without water-steeping or dew-rotting; and affords additional proof of the great advantages of the practice.

" Your Committee must also call the attention of the House to the essential benefit that will be derived to the cultivators of Flax, from the quantity of valuable food for cattle obtained from the new method of preparing Flax.

It has been given in proof, that the Boon, or outer coat of Flax, contains one-sixth of the Gluten of Oats."

*23rd May*, 1817.

---

The Machinery may be seen at work at Messrs. Hill and Bundy's Hemp and Flax Manufactory, Camden Town, near London, where Licences are granted, and every information upon the subject may be obtained.

THE END.

London: Printed by R. M'Millan,
Bow Street, Covent Garden.

# BIBLIOLIFE

## Old Books Deserve a New Life
www.bibliolife.com

Did you know that you can get most of our titles in our trademark **EasyScript**™ print format? **EasyScript**™ provides readers with a larger than average typeface, for a reading experience that's easier on the eyes.

Did you know that we have an ever-growing collection of books in many languages?

Order online:
www.bibliolife.com/store

Or to exclusively browse our **EasyScript**™ collection:
www.bibliogrande.com

At BiblioLife, we aim to make knowledge more accessible by making thousands of titles available to you – quickly and affordably.

Contact us:
BiblioLife
PO Box 21206
Charleston, SC 29413

Printed in Great Britain
by Amazon

75573453R00031